Part One : The GER and LNER Period

The line linking Loughton with Ongar dates back to 1865 and has a fascinating history.

Its story started in 1856, when the Eastern Counties Railway constructed a branch from Stratford to Loughton, with intermediate stations at Low Leyton, Snaresbrook, George Lane, Woodford and Buckhurst Hill. The terminus at Loughton stood east of the High Road and comprised two platforms. Beyond these, the tracks continued a short distance northwards and ended at a small two-road coal yard.

Loughton was destined to remain the branch terminus for nine years, although in 1858, an organisation, named the Epping Railways Company, proposed a scheme which would see the route extended to Chipping Ongar. This received Parliamentary authority during the following year, but before work commenced, the promoters announced that they wanted to extend the branch even further and take it into Dunmow. The Eastern Counties Railway objected to this idea and effectively blocked it by planning a line from Braintree to Bishops Stortford, which would serve Dunmow *en-route*. This scheme received Parliamentary sanction in 1861, but a year later the Epping Company was taken over by the Eastern Counties Railway and therefore no longer posed a territorial threat. Soon after, the ECR amalgamated with the Eastern Union Railway and, along with other companies, formed the Great Eastern Railway.

Almost immedi[...] [...]ghton - Ongar proje[...] [...]ct was awarded to t[...] [...]ugust 1862.

The new line [...] [...] quarter of a mile south of t[...] [...]us and was single track throughout [...] [...]ing loops were planned at both Epping an[...] [...]don. Apart from these, stations were constructed at Chigwell Road, North Weald, Blake Hall and Ongar. A new station was also built at Loughton to replace the earlier terminus and this, along with the rest of the line, was brought into public use on Monday 24th April 1865.

The opening ceremony seems to have been a very low-key affair, although a group of cadets from a local grammar school assembled at Ongar station and fired a rifle volley to welcome the first train as it arrived. Unfortunately, towards the close of service, the locomotive hauling the last down train became derailed at North Weald and passengers travelling to Ongar endured a delay of over eight hours.

Although much of the area served by the line remained rural, the traffic developed and, in time the GER decided that the track between Loughton and Epping should be doubled. This took place in 1892 and was operational from January 1893, but the continuation to Ongar remained single.

A view from 1911, showing the junction at Loughton, with a locomotive standing on the route of 1856 and the line towards Epping and Ongar diverging to the right. The old terminus, which stood near the future site of Lopping Hall, was demolished after closure in 1865 and its tracks were subsequently lifted. However, much of the line to its south was retained and used to serve a goods yard and carriage sidings.

Prior to opening, the extension was inspected by Captain H.W. Tyler on behalf of the Board of Trade and his report dated 10th April 1865 referred to a *"proposed excursion platform"* adjoining the goods yard. Details of this are scant, although it seems that some excursion trains terminated at or near the carriage sidings and passengers detrained onto the public road by way of a brick building. This practice probably ceased in the 1870s and the excursion facilities fell into disuse. By the early years of the twentieth century, some people seem to have erroneously assumed that this building had once been part of the original terminus and it became known locally as "the old station".

The two platforms of the 1865 station can be seen to the right.

GER Official

In the grouping of January 1923, the GER became part of the London & North Eastern Railway and this view shows the exterior of Loughton station as it appeared in LNER days.

In common with other stations on the Ongar Extension, Loughton was designed in the GER Engineer's Office under the direction of Robert Sinclair. The buildings were largely constructed in a standard style, with a double storey station master's house and adjoining offices. Today these buildings are referred to as the '1865 type' and are categorised as 'small' medium' or 'large' depending on the size of the station offices. Loughton was a fine example of the 'large type' and is seen here on 26th July 1938.

LNER Official

Having entered through the booking office, passengers found themselves on the down platform which is seen here in 1938. As built in 1865, the platforms were shorter and afforded little in the way of shelter for waiting passengers. They were lengthened around 1875 and in September 1882 that on the down side was raised in height from 2 to 3 feet. Eventually it was decided to provide extra covered accommodation for this platform, and an awning was added in 1905-6.

LNER Official

This is the up platform, viewed from the London end, again in the 1930s. It was originally narrower, but was widened in 1896, when it was provided with new buildings and the awning shown here.

LNER Official

Here we have a general view of Loughton station, looking towards London in May 1938, with the up platform on the left and the down on the right. Providing a link between them is a passenger footbridge which was erected in 1880. An ex-GER 2-4-2T stands in the dock and sports an 'Ongar' destination board, whilst behind her it is just possible to make out a vehicle standing in the carriage sidings.

LNER Official

The first station north-east of Loughton was named Chigwell Road and opened with the Ongar extension on 24th April 1865. It was of the 'Small 1865' type and originally comprised a single platform. It was renamed Chigwell Lane on 1st December 1865 and received a second platform when the track was doubled late in 1892. Traffic was light for many years and it closed as a wartime economy measure between 22nd May 1916 and 3rd February 1919. This view dates from the 1930s and shows the entrance side of the main building. *LNER Official*

This photograph looks towards Ongar and shows Chigwell Lane station in 1911. It was taken from the footbridge which was erected around the time of widening and includes the goods yard behind the down platform on the left. The bridge was constructed of wrought iron on cast pillars. The up side building was added in 1892 and its awning, seen in the right foreground was of a design frequently used by the GER around that time. The signal box, visible beyond the end of the up platform, accommodated twenty-two levers and dated from 1887.

GER Official

Left : Continuing beyond Chigwell Lane, the line reached Theydon. It was renamed Theydon Bois on 1st December 1865, so both this and Chigwell Road underwent name changes on the same date. It was built as a two-platform station so as to serve a passing loop, although the loop was not operational until 1884. The platform canopies were also added in 1884 whilst the passenger footbridge, seen beyond the buildings, was authorised towards the end of the same year. The station house was of the 'Medium 1865' type and the photograph dates from 3rd April 1937.
H.C. Casserley

Ex-GER Class F5 2-4-2T No 7143 is seen entering Theydon Bois station with an up train on 3rd April 1937. The track leading into the goods yard can be seen to the left, whilst just out of shot to the right lies the site of the old signal box, which dated from 1884-5 and was resited to the south in 1933. The locomotive had been built at Stratford Works in June 1903 and remained in service until 30th November 1955, when she ended her days as British Railways No 67190.
H.C. Casserley

Left : This view shows the approach to Epping station from the London end and was taken on 8th May 1911. The sidings on the left belonged to the goods yard, which partly dated from the line's opening in 1865, but was subsequently enlarged in 1893. To serve connections into the enlarged depot, the GER erected a small ground frame on the up side of the running lines and this can be seen to the right. Behind this stands the Epping Gasworks and this had a private siding which had existed since the early days of the branch. The curving platforms of the passenger station are visible in the distance, whilst in the left foreground lie some well tended allotments.
GER Official

Epping station opened with the line on 24th April 1865 and comprised two platforms from the outset. The photograph reproduced here was taken from an Edwardian commercial postcard and looks towards Ongar from the London end of the down platform. The signal box on the left dated from 1887, whilst the passenger footbridge beyond was added in 1891-2 at a cost of £384. Fashions displayed by the passengers intending to board the in-coming up train add to the period atmosphere.

T.E. Atkins collection

The main building at Epping was constructed in red brick and was of the 'Large 1865' type. This view, which was taken in August 1935, includes a good display of LNER poster boards and a public telephone box, just visible to the right.

London Transport Museum

Epping station, looking towards London in April 1938. Both platforms had been lengthened at either end since opening and the end of the wall indicates the north-eastern extent of the up side when built in 1865. The footbridge had originally carried a roof, but this had been removed by the time that the photo was taken.

LNER Official

For this view, the LNER photographer stood on the footbridge at Epping and pointed his camera towards London. There seems to be little in the way of activity apart from five young men on the down platform, who might possibly have been enthusiasts. Three of them are certainly intently interested in something which appears to be fairly small. Could they have been collecting tickets and found that the booking office still had some pre-grouping issues in its racks, or had they discovered a luggage label to some long-closed station? Such conjecture aside however, the photograph gives us a good view of the station buildings on both sides and includes part of the gasworks in the distance.

LNER Official

This is the little locomotive shed at Epping, as it appeared on 12th May 1938. It dated from 1893 and comprised two roads. The shed was rebuilt in 1949.

LNER Official

Beyond Epping the line was less busy and epitomised the country branch. This view shows the exterior of North Weald station as it appeared in the 1930s, with a GER 'Small Type' 1865 building and the goods yard entrance on the right. North Weald was some distance from the nearest public road, so a 250 yard approach road had to be constructed to provide access.

Above : This photograph looks towards North Weald station, with its 270ft long platform, and includes the signal box which dated from 1888. The adjoining track was a siding accessed from the Epping end, although prior to 1888 it could be reached from the Ongar end as well. As can be seen, an occupation crossing existed at the station's eastern end, although this was only intended as a footpath.
LNER Official

Right : Like North Weald, Blake Hall was a typical country station and led a quiet existence since it opened with the line in 1865. This photograph was taken from a signal post in May 1911 and shows its layout from the Epping end. The goods yard can be seen on the left, whilst to the right stands the signal box, which was built in 1888.
GER Official

A photograph from the road bridge gives us a good view of Blake Hall station at an unknown date. The building was of the 1865 'Small Type' and was constructed of red brick with white dressings.

Photographer unknown

This is the approach to Ongar, as it appeared on 9th May 1911. The passenger station stands directly ahead, beyond the signal box, whilst the engine shed and associated tracks lie to the left and the goods yard lies to the right. The parapets in the foreground are the beginning of the viaduct over Cripsey Brook. *GER Official*

As befitted the branch terminus, Ongar station was provided with an 1865 'Large type' building and is seen here from the Station Approach in the 1930s. The gates on the left led into the goods yard, and behind these can be seen some cattle pens .

LNER Official

Although constructed as a terminus, Ongar was laid out very much in the style of a through station, perhaps in the hope that the line might have been extended in the direction of Dunmow at some time. The platform was originally 350ft long, but was extended at its western end in 1891 to increase its length to 470ft. The photograph was taken on 12th May 1938. The track in the foreground was the run-round loop, whilst that branching off to the right served the locomotive shed, being used to unload loco coal.

LNER Official

The signal box near the London end of the platform at Ongar, again dated from 1888, and controlled movements around the station and yard. The building to the right is the engine shed, which was built in 1865 and contained a single road. This photograph, which also includes the locomotive water tank, was taken on 11th June 1938.

H.C. Casserley

This photograph gives us a view of the complete engine shed, taken from its western end on 11th June 1938, with the passenger station to the right. The shed was demolished in 1943, although the siding and pit remained in-situ.

H.C. Casserley

Ongar goods yard is seen in 1911, with the goods shed at centre and four staff cottages in the distance to the right. These were erected in 1892 and, along with seven others that were built opposite them in 1912, are still standing in Banson's Way.

GER Official

Ex-GER Class F5 2-4-2T No 7144 prepares for departure from Ongar on 11th June 1938. Her classmate, No 7147 stands beside piles of discarded ash outside the engine shed on the left, also carrying a 'Liverpool Street' destination board on her bunker. Both locomotives were built in 1903 and were withdrawn in 1955 and 1957 respectively.

H.C. Casserley

Part Two : The London Transport Period

On 5th June 1935, the Government announced a £35,000,000 scheme to improve various sections of the railway network around London. The work was expected to be completed within five years and included electrifying some of the suburban lines serving Essex.

Of these, the route to Shenfield was to be electrified and operated by the LNER, whilst services between Stratford and Ongar, along with the Hainault Loop would be transferred to the London Passenger Transport Board.

Under the scheme, the Central London tube line was to be extended eastwards in tunnel from Liverpool Street, through Bethnal Green and Mile End to Stratford, where it would surface at the existing LNER station. Beyond here, the route would again descend into tunnel, then join the Ongar branch a little to the south of Leyton.

As part of the plan, both Stratford and Loughton stations would be extensively rebuilt.

In readiness for the forthcoming changes, the LPTB Central London Line, had its name shortened to the Central Line on 28th August 1937.

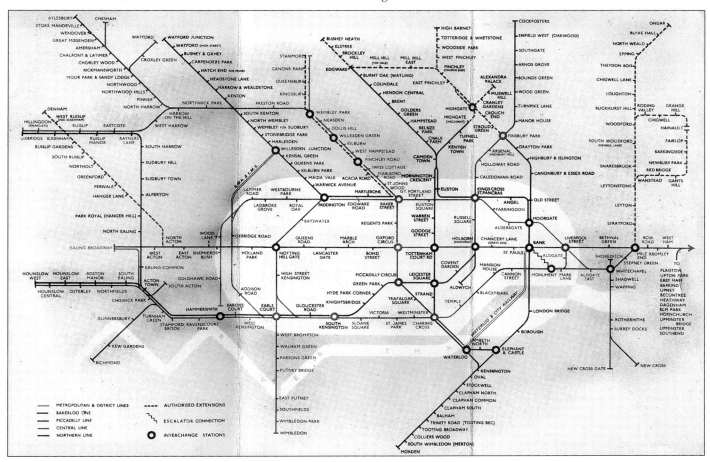

The first LPTB pocket map to include the various new extensions appeared in 1938 with new, or newly electrified routes indicated as "under construction".

Tube trains serving stations towards Ongar, would utilise the old Great Eastern line from Leyton, but a completely new connection was to be built in tunnel, linking Leytonstone with Newbury Park on the Hainault Loop. With this in position, it would be possible to close the former GER route linking Newbury Park with Ilford and Seven Kings and incorporate the loop into the Tube network.

Before all this could take place however, it was necessary to construct the new tunnels and carry out various changes to the existing infrastructure.

Some of this work had been completed by the outbreak of the Second World War in September 1939 and, for a while, the LPTB seemed optimistic that all would be completed as planned. A pocket folding map issued in the second half of 1939 listed the various "Future Extensions" under the hopeful heading "New In London", but although the earliest of these indeed materialised, the others were either delayed by the war or, in some cases, scrapped completely.

Both : J.E. Connor collection

FUTURE EXTENSIONS

1939

AUTUMN. BAKERLOO LINE. Baker Street to Finchley Road : through trains between Elephant & Castle and Stanmore.

1940

SPRING. NORTHERN LINE. East Finchley to High Barnet : through trains between High Barnet and Morden.

SPRING. CENTRAL LINE. North Acton to Greenford : through trains between Greenford and Liverpool Street.

SPRING. CENTRAL LINE. Liverpool Street to Loughton and Hainault (via Woodford) : through trains between Greenford, Loughton and Hainault.

SUMMER. CENTRAL LINE. Greenford to Ruislip : through trains between Ruislip and Loughton.

AUTUMN. NORTHERN LINE. Drayton Park to Alexandra Palace : through trains between Alexandra Palace and High Barnet and Moorgate.

1941

SPRING. CENTRAL LINE. Loughton to Ongar : and Leytonstone to Woodford via Newbury Park : through trains, Loughton, Hainault and Ruislip (via Woodford), Hainault and Ruislip (via Newbury Park).

The rebuilt station at Loughton was designed for the LNER by the architect John Murray Easton. It comprised a pair of island platforms serving three tracks and was located a little to the east of its 1865 predecessor. It is seen here whilst under construction, with the new entrance building behind the signal and a man standing near the base of the earlier down platform ramp on the left.

LNER Official

Above : The new station opened on 28th April 1940, but over eight years would elapse before the promised tube services would arrive. This undated view shows a down train departing behind a Class N7 0-6-2T.

Lens of Sutton collection

Work on modernising the line resumed after the war and tube trains were extended from Liverpool Street to Stratford on 4th December 1946. Five months later, on 5th May 1947, they reached Leytonstone, then, on 14th December 1947, a further extension saw them reach Woodford. Almost a year later, on 21st November 1948, London Transport services eventually reached Loughton, where passengers for Chigwell Lane and beyond changed into trains of steam-hauled compartment stock.

Right : **Extract from the LT pocket map of June 1949, after electric services had been extended to Loughton.**
J.E. Connor collection

Below : **Class F5 2-4-2T No 67199 awaits departure from Loughton with an Ongar line train in the late 1940s. A train of LT Standard stock can be seen to the right. No 67199 dated from November 1904 and was withdrawn on 28th February 1957.**
R.A.P Cogger

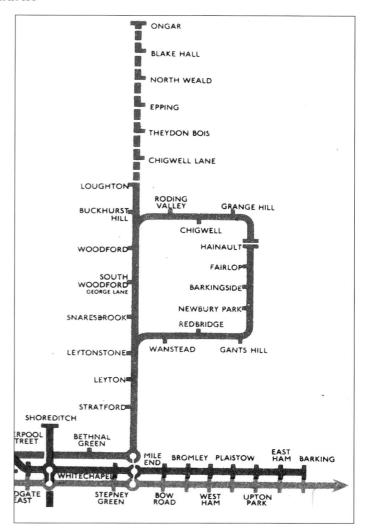

Opposite : **Loughton station, soon after electrification. At this time tube trains served the outer faces of the two platforms whilst Epping and Ongar steam services used the centre road.** *Photographer unknown*

Left : In readiness for the takeover of services by London Transport, the stations along the route were fitted with LT roundels. Those at Chigwell Lane were very short-lived however, as the station was renamed Debden on 25th September 1949, when electric trains were extended to Epping. Although rural for many years, the surrounding area was transformed into the London County Council Debden housing estate during the late 1940s and early 1950s.

Fred Ivey

Right : Extract from the LT pocket map of January 1950, after electric services had been extended to Epping and Chigwell Lane had been renamed Debden.

Passengers for Ongar would alight at Epping and change into a steam-worked shuttle service.

J.E. Connor collection

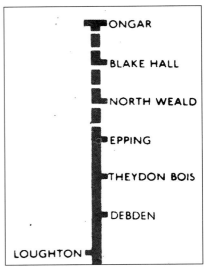

Below : A train of London Transport Standard tube stock is seen at Debden in the 1950s. With the changeover to LT, the former up line was re-designated 'Westbound' whilst the down line became 'Eastbound'.

Alan A. Jackson

Above : Steam-hauled passenger trains occasionally appeared on the line south of Epping, although they were always special workings. This view was taken from a window of one such train as it passed Loughton on 29th April 1956.

R.M. Casserley

Below : Goods trains also remained steam-hauled until diesels took over in 1962. Here we see Class J15 0-6-0 No 65455 in the yard at Loughton, some time in the 1950s. These locomotives were designed by T.W. Worsdell and introduced by the Great Eastern Railway in 1883. This particular example was built at Stratford Works in June 1906 and remained in service until 31st March 1960. After withdrawal in September 1962, classmate No 65462 was bought for preservation and is now based on the North Norfolk Railway.

Photographer unknown

Modernisation of the line between Epping and Ongar included converting the siding at North Weald into a passing loop and providing it with a platform. This was brought into use on 14th August 1949, and can be seen to the right of this view, which also includes the concrete footbridge erected to link the two platforms. The original print is undated, but the temporary roundel on the left, together with what appears to be a timetable poster headed by a British Railways totem, reflects well the period of transition.

Photographer unknown.

Class F5 2-4-2T No 67200 departs from the loop platform at North Weald on 23rd March 1957 with a train for Epping. At peak times between 1949 and 1957, there was a train every twenty minutes on this section and these crossed at North Weald. This was the busiest station north-east of Epping as it served an RAF airfield and such was the demand for forces leave tickets during holiday periods that a temporary booking office was once provided at the airfield itself. In the background, behind the train and station, can be seen the since-demolished North Weald radio masts.

EORVS collection

F5 2-4-2T No 67193 awaits departure from Ongar on 1st June 1957, with a train for Epping. The locomotives employed on the Epping-Ongar shuttles were all push-pull fitted, so there was no need to run round on completion of each journey. No 67193 was withdrawn on 30th November 1957.

M.L. Boakes collection

Another F5, this time No 67203 stands at Epping and prepares to propel her two-car push-pull set back to Ongar on 21st July 1957. The steam-worked shuttle service was now in its final days and therefore the line was proving popular with railway photographers. 67203 was withdrawn on 31st December 1957
W.E. Cooper / M.L. Boakes collection

The crew of 67200, along with another railwayman, pose for the photographer at Epping on 15th June 1957, whilst a train of Standard tube stock stands at the other platform. From a handwritten note on the original print, it appears that the loco driver was a Mr. Dearman. No 67200 was withdrawn on 11th December 1957. *Photographer unknown*

In steam days it proved necessary to have a small locomotive shed at Epping, to service engines employed on both passenger and goods trains. This view, which dates from 11th July 1953, shows ex-GER Class J15 0-6-0 No 65464, alongside ex-Great Northern Railway C12 4-4-2T No 67363. The C12 had been fitted with push-pull gear and was used briefly on branch passenger services around this time. Epping was a sub-shed of the much larger depot at Stratford and closed when the section to Ongar was electrified. *B.K.B. Green*

Tube trains began to operate between Epping and Ongar on 18th November 1957, although the service remained a shuttle. A two-car train of 1935 tube stock is seen arriving at Ongar on the first day of electric operation. In 1958, these trains were lengthened by adding a centre trailer car of Standard Stock, dating from 1927. Between 1963 and 1965, the three sets used on the branch shuttle were repainted from red to silver so they matched the 1962 Stock trains then in use on the main section of the Central Line.

F. Church

This view shows a three-car train of Standard stock leaving Ongar for Epping at an unknown date, with the track leading to the goods yard visible in the right foreground. *Photographer unknown / EORVS collection*

An additional footbridge was erected at the country end of Debden station in the mid-1950s to provide access from the housing estate to the Bank of England printing works on the opposite side of the line. This view dates from around 1959 and includes a westbound train formed of Standard stock approaching on the right. At the far end of the platform stands the LT signal cabin, which replaced the old Chigwell Lane box from 26th June 1949 and continued in use until 29th July 1996. Nearby are a pair of reversing sidings which were added by LT to accommodate trains booked to terminate at Debden. The station was partially rebuilt during 1973-4 when the entrance was modernised and new awnings were erected.

Photographer unknown / A.D. Simpson collection

On Saturday 7th April 1962, the Locomotive Club of Great Britain operated the *'Great Eastern Suburban Rail Tour'*, which was booked to leave Liverpool Street at 13.37 and visited various ex-GER branches, including Ongar. From Liverpool Street to Palace Gates and Chingford, the train was hauled by an N7 class 0-6-2T, but the remainder of the tour was worked by J15 0-6-0 No 65476. Here the train, which was limited to three carriages, is seen alongside the goods shed at Ongar, where it was booked to arrive at 17.11 and depart at 17.44. No 65476 dated from August 1908 and was withdrawn on 30th September 1962.

Photographer unknown / M. L. Boakes collection

The three trains of 1935/27 Stock were withdrawn by the end of 1966 and replaced by aluminium-finish 1962 Stock as seen here at Ongar. The signal box had closed on 23rd March 1969, having outlived the goods yard by three years, and was subsequently demolished.

Photographer unknown / EORVS collection

Top : Looking towards Epping station from the country end at an unknown date. Generally, trains to and from central London used platform 2, on the right, whilst the Ongar shuttle operated out of platform 1, although there were exceptions.

Photographer unknown/ EORVS collection

Middle : A train of 1962 Stock stands by the seemingly empty platform at Ongar, awaiting departure. Traffic over the section between Epping and Ongar was so light that it was proposed for complete closure by London Transport in 1970. After agreeing a scheme of subsidisation with Essex County Council however, the line was spared, although, for economic reasons, a 'one train' service was introduced from 18th October 1976, when North Weald box was switched out. After this there was no further need for the passing loop at North Weald, so it was lifted during July 1978. *D.J. Bowker*

Below : Blake Hall had the unenviable but not unexpected distinction of being the quietest station on the LT system with an average of six passengers a day, and lost its Sunday services in 1966. Its goods yard closed from 18th April that year and its track was subsequently lifted. *D. J. Bowker*

The Essex County Council subsidy ended in 1977 and complete closure was again threatened three years later. The branch itself received a further reprieve although the little used station at Blake Hall was not so lucky and closed after traffic on Saturday 31st October 1981.

These views show the ticket hall interior on the last day, with that above looking onto the platform and that below facing the forecourt.

As would be expected, many railway enthusiasts attended, although for most of the day there were not the crowds evident at some other closures.

Nevertheless, the booking office, seen in the upper photograph, was busy selling last day edmondson tickets and, until supplies dried up, handing out the then current LT folding 'Journey Planner' maps, endorsed with the station's rubber stamp.

Both : J.E. Connor

Above : The two types of closure notice displayed at Blake Hall station on its last day.

Below : The station building on the same date, with an impressive display of closure notices. As can be seen, all windows had been boarded up except those in the station house. *Both J.E. Connor*

Right : On its final day, Blake Hall station only retained the roundel in front of the building, as that near the Epping end of the platform had already been removed.

Middle : Blake Hall station viewed from the from bridge at its Ongar end, with a few enthusiasts in attendance. The main building was granted Grade II listed status in April 1984 and is now a private house.

Bottom : A train of 1962 Stock calls at Blake Hall on the last night of passenger services in October 1981.

All: J.E. Connor

The train service linking Epping with Ongar was reduced to working during the Monday - Friday peak periods only from 6th December 1982. This continued until 30th October 1989, when an all-week timetable was restored, but there was little demand and closure became inevitable.

The last London Transport train to operate between Epping and Ongar ran on Friday 30th September 1994. It was formed of red-painted 1960 Stock cars Nos 3906 and 3907, running with 1938 Stock trailer No 4927. It operated during the evening peak and is seen at Epping, carrying a 'Last Train' headboard, along with a roundel behind the off-side cab window displaying the legend "The Silent Whistle. Epping - Ongar". *J.E. Connor*

The last evening of LT services at Ongar saw enthusiasts and others gathering at the station waiting to travel on, or just watch, the final train. As can be seen, at least one of the platform roundels had already been removed. *J.E. Connor*

Right : The last LT departure from Ongar left at around 19.15 and is shown just before setting out. The three-car unit was crowded to say the least!

Middle : The other end of the train seen as it paused at North Weald. The disused and trackless loop platform is visible on the left.

Bottom (left) : North Weald station building on 30th September 1994, after the last LT train had departed. An era may have ended, but, in time, a new one would begin.

Bottom (right) : The directional sign near the commencement of the station approach, again recorded on the last night of London Transport services.

All : J.E. Connor

Part Three : The preservation era

Prior to closure, the Ongar Railway Preservation Society was formed, with a view to acquire the line beyond Epping and operate it with both tube and locomotive-hauled stock. Around 1997 however, the branch was bought by a commercial organisation instead. It was hoped that a commuter service would be restored, but changes to the signalling system at Epping would have made this difficult and no trains ran. This view shows Ongar station soon after closure, before the electric conductor rails were lifted. *EORVS Collection*

In addition to the planned commuter services, the new owners stated their intention to attract tourists by running steam-hauled trains. To operate these, the company purchased some locomotives and stock of Finnish origin, but as these were built to a slightly wider gauge, they could not be used without extensive track alterations.

Left (upper) : A line-up of Finnish locomotives and stock at Ongar, led by 0-6-0T No 794, followed by 2-8-0 No 1134 and a 4-6-2. *Michael Hardy*

Left (lower) : The line-up, viewed from the opposite end, with a 2-8-2 in the foreground. *Michael Hardy*

The early twenty-first century saw the creation of the Epping Ongar Railway Volunteer Society, which started out as a small group of enthusiasts banding together to help preserve the line's buildings and track. A Class 117 diesel multiple unit was acquired and brought into service on 10th October 2004, when it carried passengers between Ongar and North Weald. After the winter of 2005, it became possible to extend operations to Coopersale, east of Epping, when the trackbed beneath the M11 bridge was lowered. This bridge had been erected in the 1970s and, of course, was only designed for tube height trains to pass underneath it. Here the Class 117 unit is seen alongside the Finnish 4-6-2 in July 2006.

EORVS Collection

In April 2007, 2-8-0 No 1151 was steamed and operated over a short section of 5ft gauge track at Ongar, but by this time, more changes were in the offing and the majority of the Finnish locomotives would soon be dispersed to other locations.

In December 2007 a further change of ownership came and today's Epping Ongar Railway was born.

There was clearly a great deal of work to be done and, although the new organisation had no income at the time, a private benefactor came forward to finance materials.

The Epping Ongar Railway Volunteers Society came into its own by providing the workforce, and contractors were employed to cover the tasks which the membership were unable to carry out.

Now, work on transforming the line could begin in earnest.

Michael Hardy

In December 2007 the track at Ongar included just a basic headshunt and siding, whilst the Finnish stock was stored on the site of the erstwhile run-round loop. As part of the new scheme, 300 metres of track between the buffer stops and the viaduct west of the station was lifted and new drainage was installed. Within the station area, the trackbed had been raised at the time of electrification, so that tube trains could be accommodated at the platform. All this had to be dug out, so that the track could be lowered to suit the needs of standard height stock and, where possible the layout was to be restored to a semblance of its original formation. Track was re-laid into the old milk and cattle docks, to be used as storage sidings, but nothing could be done with the former goods yard area, as the site had by then been sold for development. This view shows work under way and includes the temporary engine shed on the left, which incorporates the original locomotive pit.

EORVS Collection

As can be seen from this view, a temporary nameboard had been added by the previous owners to a frame vacated by one of the station's London Transport roundels around the time of closure in 1994. This was soon to disappear however, as the EOR intended to restore Ongar station to its Great Eastern Railway appearance, with original paint samples being measured by a colorimeter to ensure their accurate reproduction.

The main building had been granted Grade II listed status in July 1984, but it had fallen into disrepair and much remedial work had to be done before it could be reopened.

The train behind the platform wall is a two car 'Hampshire' diesel multiple unit, introduced to the Southern Region of British Railways in 1957 and latterly referred to as Class 205, although unofficially they were known as 'Thumpers'.

EORVS Collection

The trackbed at North Weald had also been raised in LT days and therefore required lowering to befit its new role. This view shows contractors at work and includes the original signal box on the left. Restoration of this started in 2006, before the change of ownership, but its fabric was badly deteriorated and much still needed doing. The original stairs to the operating and locking rooms had rotted and were unsafe, so they had to be completely replaced by the volunteer workforce. The glazing was also in a bad way and the windows had been boarded up to prevent further decay and vandalism.

The station building also suffered from neglect and had to be thoroughly renovated. Internally, a ticket machine room had to be demolished to allow the booking hall to be restored to its original layout and the ladies' toilet was brought back into use, having previously been converted for storage.

Both : *EORVS Collection*

The former up platform at North Weald had been constructed on a bed which was largely formed of ash and clinker. In time, this had settled and the surface began to crack. The attendant concrete shelter suffered extensive spalling and, at the end, it was apparently only being held together by its metal reinforcing bars, The shelter was subsequently demolished after being declared unsafe and much of the platform had to undergo rebuilding.

EORVS Collection

Above : Volunteers at work, restoring the signal box at North Weald.

Left : Track laying taking place at North Weald. Although much of the task of restoring the railway was handled by volunteers, work such as driving diggers and cranes had to be performed by contractors.

Both : EORVS Collection

The 1949 concrete footbridge at North Weald was also badly decayed and needed to be replaced. To do this, the EOR were presented with a Great Eastern Railway lattice iron bridge which had been removed from Churchfields, near South Woodford in 1999. Unfortunately, the stairs became damaged whilst the bridge was being dismantled.

Above : The supporting columns outside the station building at North Weald.

Right (upper) : The span after removal to North Weald, along with sections of prefabricated track, which had been lifted from the vicinity of Custom House station, on the North Woolwich branch.

Right (lower) : A view from the east end of North Weald station, showing newly laid track, along with footbridge columns on the right and crossing gates on the left. These gates, which protect the former occupation crossing, were acquired from Chitt's Hill, on the London side of Colchester. Chitt's Hill was the last manually worked crossing on the Norwich main line and the gates became redundant as part of a resignalling scheme.

All : EORVS Collection

As the original signal box at Ongar was demolished many years ago, it was necessary to acquire one from elsewhere. To ensure accuracy it had to be one of the same type and fortunately a suitable redundant cabin was found at Spellbrook, near Bishop's Stortford. It was duly dismantled and the top was taken by road to Mangapps Railway Museum. Subsequently it was moved to Ongar where it is shown after arrival.

Top : The upper section of the former Spellbrook signal box after arrival at Ongar. The new nameboard was fitted before it set out on its journey.

Above : The interior of the box as it appeared on arrival. Luckily, the frame from Ongar survived in private hands and has since been reinstalled.

Left : As part of the station restoration at Ongar, an original GER fireplace was sourced and, after sandblasting with fine grit, was installed in the booking hall. The company crest was subsequently re-painted by a volunteer signwriter and provides a delightful finishing touch.

All EORVS Collection

Eventually, all the hard work paid off and on 25th May 2012, steam-hauled passenger trains returned to the branch. Here we see ex-Great Western Railway 49xx class 4-6-0 No 4953 *'Pitchford Hall'* at the reopening ceremony, breaking through a banner which had been strung above the tracks at North Weald. The EOR is the closest heritage railway to the capital and the event was covered by both BBC London and BBC Essex. In a press release, Roger Wright, Director of the Epping Ongar Railway stated that *"The extensive works on the restoration of the track, signals, stations and rolling stock undertaken by volunteers aged from 18 to 82 has been key to the return of steam to the railway"*.

EORVS Collection

These two photographs were taken in June 2012 and look towards the buffer stops at Ongar.

The upper view includes the erstwhile Spellbrook signal box in the foreground, which by then had been completely transformed.

After arrival on site its upper half was provided with a new lower section and thoroughly restored. The roof was re-slated, using original slates for one face and salvaged slates for the other. The window and wall panel assembly at one end had to be completely renewed as it much of the original was either missing or rotten. Once the structure had been repaired, all of its exterior wood was rubbed down, made good and painted. New stairs and a balcony were constructed, but as Spellbrook had lost its original balcony brackets, these had to be sourced elsewhere. A single GE-pattern bracket was acquired from the old Enfield Town box and from this accurate copies were made to complete the balcony. The original signalman's door was restored and re-fitted, whilst down below, in the new lower section, a locking room door from Custom House was bought and installed.

The lower photograph shows the refurbished lever frame, which after arrival at Ongar was dismantled, restored and reassembled, with some of the levers rearranged to fit in with new signalling arrangements.

Top : J.E. Connor.
Bottom : EORVS Collection

Ongar station looking towards thew buffer stops in June 2012.

The Grade II listed main building has been beautifully restored, as have the adjoining porters' room and footwarmer hut. Over the years, the porters' room had lost many of its slates and its windows were broken. During restoration, it was provided with replacement roofing slates, re-glazed and plastered internally, as much of the original plaster was missing. The footwarmer hut also had new glazing fitted and the brickwork was re-pointed. *J.E. Connor*

The station at Blake Hall had been converted into a private house and lost its platform in LT days. It therefore remains closed, but can be seen from passing trains, as in this photograph, which was taken in June 2012.

J.E. Connor

North Weald has also been nicely restored and now includes locomotive facilities behind the Epping end of the down platform. During its rehabilitation, the station building was re-wired by having its LT surface ducting removed and having new cabling installed within the walls. West of here, the EOR operate trains. From April 2015, past Coopersale into Epping Forest, just a few hundred yards from Epping station. The train standing in Platform 2 is a diesel-hauled North Weald - Coopersale shuttle, formed of ex-Southern Region 3CIG unit no 1498.

J.E. Connor

A resident on the Epping Ongar Railway is ex-GWR 49xx class 4-6-0 No 4953 'Pitchford Hall'. She belongs to a once numerous class of mixed traffic locomotives which were designed by the GWR Chief Mechanical Engineer, Mr C.B. Collett, and was built at Swindon Works in the summer of 1929. She remained in service until spring 1963 when she was withdrawn and, soon after was sold for scrap to Woodham Brothers of Barry. Fortunately the company were kept busy cutting up other items and 'Pitchford Hall', like numerous other condemned locomotives remained untouched. Eventually she was bought for preservation in February 1984 and restored to full working order.

The view above shows her departing from Ongar in June 2012, whilst below she is seen after arrival at North Weald.

Both : J.E. Connor

Top : English Electric Type 3, now known as Class 37, No D6729, resplendent in BR green livery, stands at North Weald in June 2012.

Above (left) : Ex-Southern Region 3-CIG unit No 1498 stands at North Weald in June 2012.

Above (right) : Ex-Southern Region 'Hampshire' DMU, now known as Class 205, awaits restoration at North Weald in 2013. The unit has since been repainted in Network SouthEast livery.

Left : Hawthorn Leslie 0-6-0ST 'Isabel' was built in 1919 as works number 3437 and worked for ICI at their Brackley plant until withdrawn in 1969. She was the first EOR steam locomotive to arrive on the line and is currently being overhauled by volunteers.

All : J.E. Connor

Passengers travelling to the Epping Ongar Railway by public transport can reach the line by means of two vintage 'bus routes and enjoy a journey on vehicles such as those seen here. At the time of writing, Route 339 provides a link with both Epping and Shenfield, whilst 381 runs during the summer from Epping to North Weald via scenic country lanes.

Above : RTL1076 stands at North Weald in 2012. The RTL class were introduced by London Transport in 1948 and were a Leyland-engined version of the RT class.

Right : Green liveried RT1700 arrives at North Weald from Epping in 2012.

Below : RF401 at North Weald in 2013. These LT single-deckers were introduced in 1951.   *All : J.E. Connor*

In 2013, the London Underground system celebrated its 150th anniversary, as the initial section of the Metropolitan Railway opened between Farringdon Street and Bishop's Road, Paddington in January 1863. This event was marked on the Epping Ongar Railway by a special gala held in the summer, using locomotives connected with the Metropolitan Railway. Foremost of these was E class 0-4-4T No 1, which had been designed by Mr T.F. Clark and built at Neasden Works in 1898. Perhaps the highlight of her early career was when she worked the first train into the original Metropolitan terminus at Uxbridge in 1904, decorated with flags, bunting and whitewashed coal. The top view shows her at Ongar, whilst that below was taken on the approach to North Weald.

Both : J.E. Connor

Mr H.N. (later Sir Nigel) Gresley's N2 class 0-6-2Ts were introduced by the Great Northern Railway towards the end of 1920, and used intensively on the suburban lines out of King's Cross. They were fitted with condensing apparatus as they regularly worked through the Metropolitan City Widened Lines tunnels linking the GN with Moorgate Street. No 1744, which dated from February 1921, ended her working life as BR 69523 in September 1962 and was subsequently bought for preservation by the Gresley Society. In the view above she is seen awaiting departure from North Weald, and below she is passing Blake Hall, where a short section of platform has been reinstated, although not for public use. No 1744 will be based on the EOR during the summer of 2015.

Both : J.E. Connor

Resident locomotive, ex-GWR 2-6-2T No 4141 appeared at the Underground gala but was disguised as No 6141.

4141 is a member of the 5101 class and was built to a C.B. Collett design of 1929 in August 1946. Her working life was spent around Gloucester and she was withdrawn for scrapping in February 1963. No 4141 spent some time in the yard of Woodham Brothers in Barry, before being bought and moved to the Severn Valley Railway in January 1973. The 5101s were similar in most respects to the 61xx class, which were a type once familiar on London suburban services out of Paddington. Therefore, in keeping with the London theme, No 4141 was temporarily renumbered.

The view above shows her running-round at Ongar, resplendent in BR green livery with polished copper-capped chimney and brass safety valve bonnet. The photograph below records '6141' with a train including ex-LT stock. The Metropolitan Railway 4-wheel coach next to the engine was loaned from the London Transport Museum and proved popular with visitors.

Both : J.E. Connor

The other steam locomotive used on the EOR during the 'Underground 150' gala was 2-6-2T No L150. This is an ex-GWR 2-6-2T of the 4575 class, which was built in December 1927 and was originally numbered 5521.

During her career for the GWR and BR, she was based at Newton Abbott, Taunton, Machynlleth, St Blazey and Laira, amongst others. She was withdrawn in April 1962 and sold to Woodham Brothers of Barry as scrap. No 5521 was bought for preservation in the autumn of 1975 and was subsequently moved to the Dean Forest Railway where she was restored to working order.

In April 2007, No 5521 was placed on a ship and travelled from Hull to Gdynia in Poland. She appeared in locomotive parades held at Wolsztyn in 2007, 8 and 9, and also worked in Hungary and Slovakia. Her time in eastern Europe also included a spell on suburban services out of Wroclaw, Poland, before returning to England.

In May 2013, she was painted in London Transport red at the request of London Underground, and received the number L150 in recognition of the anniversary.

The locomotive is fitted with a Westinghouse pump on the right side so she can work with either vacuum or air-braked stock.

The views reproduced here show L150 at Blake Hall (top) and North Weald (middle and bottom). *All : J.E. Connor*

The 2014 steam gala brought three more visitors to the line, including this ex-London & South Western Railway 2-4-0WT No 30585. She is from a class of locomotives, designed by Joseph Beattie and introduced in 1863. Eighty five of them were built, but most were withdrawn towards the end of the nineteenth century. Amazingly, three survived into British Railways ownership in 1948 however and were retained for working the Wenford Bridge branch until 1962. In their earliest years the 'Beattie Well Tanks' as they were known, were used on London suburban services, but, as trains became heavier, they proved under-powered. Two of them, 30585 and 30587 made a welcome return to London in December 1962 to work a couple of Railway Correspondence and Travel Society special trains from Waterloo.

The view above shows 30585 running light at North Weald, whilst below, she is standing at North Weald station, awaiting departure with the 14.00 train to Ongar on 6th June 2014. *Both : J.E. Connor*

Another star of the 2014 steam gala was ex-LMSR 'Standard Goods' 0-6-0T No 47408. These locomotives, generally referred to by enthusiasts as 'Jinties', were a post-grouping development of an S.W. Johnson Midland Railway design and were built during the period that Sir Henry Fowler was Chief Mechanical Engineer. They were very successful and could be found all over the LMS system. They were primarily intended for goods work, although the class was also used at times to work passenger trains. In the London area, these largely comprised the steam-hauled services linking Broad Street with Poplar and destinations on the former GNR. No 47406 was built as LMS No 16489 in 1926 and was withdrawn in December 1966. She was bought as scrap by Woodhams Brothers, but after rusting in the yard at Barry for many years was re-sold for preservation in 1983.

The top photograph was taken at North Weald and the bottom shows her arriving at Ongar.

Both : J.E. Connor

Another ex-LMSR stalwart performing in the 2014 EOR steam gala was 5MT 4-6-0 No 45379. This class was designed by Mr W.A. (later Sir William) Stanier and first appeared in 1934. As their 'MT' power classification indicates, they were intended for mixed traffic work and therefore were turned out in lined-black livery. To differentiate them from the larger wheeled express passenger 5XP 'Jubilee' class which was painted in LMSR red, they were quickly dubbed 'Black Fives' and this nickname has stuck with them ever since. Again, a very numerous class and arguably one of the most successful of British steam locomotives. Some of them remained in service until 1968. 45379 was built in July 1937 and was allocated to various sheds before being sent to Willesden in March 1964. Here she remained until withdrawal the following year and was one of the last locomotives to leave after the depot closed. She went to Barry scrapyard in October 1965, but survived and was bought for preservation in May 1974.

Both photographs show her at North Weald, with that below including 5101 class 2-6-2T No 4141.

Both : J.E. Connor

The 1960 Stock train which worked the last London Underground services in and out of Ongar in September 1994, returned to the line twenty years later to take part in a commemorative gala.

The unit, with a pair of Schoma diesels at either end, crossed the boundary between LUL and the EOR at Epping at around 02.30 on the morning of 26th September 2014, and continued to North Weald. Later that morning, at 09.30, crowds gathered at Ongar to watch the first tube train since 1994 to arrive at the station.

The event was extremely popular and the 1960 Stock unit was filled to capacity on some of its trips.

Ex-Metropolitan Railway E Class 0-4-4T No 1 made a return visit to the branch and operated demonstration engineers' trains at North Weald, as well as hauling some of the passenger services.

Right : The 1960 tube stock train, with two LUL Schoma diesel locomotives in the foreground await at Epping, prior to crossing onto the EOR.   *O. Hayward*

Below : The 1960 Stock unit, owned by Craven Heritage Trains, is seen at North Weald.   *EORVS*

A SELECTION OF THE LINE'S DIESEL LOCOMOTIVES *Top left :* 03119, formerly D2119. *Top right :* 03170, formerly D2170. *Middle left :* D7523. *Middle right :* 31438. *Bottom left :* 45132, formerly D22. *Bottom right :* 47635 *'Jimmy Milne'*, formerly D1606.

All photographs EORVS Collection, except middle right J. Cross and bottom right P. Chester